What Rules Should We Have in Our Classroom?

by Mrs. DeLaSierra's class
with Tony Stead

1. Be a good listener.
2.
3.
4.

capstone® classroom

Rules are important to have in the classroom.

4

We think that these rules are very important to have in our classroom.

Rule One: Be a good listener.

This rule is important because an adult could be telling us something we need to know about, and we learn from each other.

Rule Two: Follow directions.

We think this rule is important because we need to be safe, and we need to know what to do in class.

Rules are important to have so that everyone feels safe and happy. What rules do you think are important to have in your classroom?